DIGITAL AND INFORMATION LITERACY ™

PHYSICAL
COMPUTING AND
MAKERSPACES

AMIE JANE LEAVITT

rosen publishing's
rosen central®

New York

Published in 2015 by The Rosen Publishing Group, Inc.
29 East 21st Street, New York, NY 10010

Library of Congress Cataloging-in-Publication Data

Leavitt, Amie Jane.
Physical computing and makerspaces/Amie Leavitt.
    pages cm. — (Digital and information literacy)
Audience: Grades 5-8.
Includes bibliographical references and index.
ISBN 978-1-4777-7659-9 (library bound) — ISBN 978-1-4777-7661-2 (pbk.)
— ISBN 978-1-4777-7662-9 (6-pack)
1. Makerspaces—Juvenile literature. 2. Inventions—Juvenile literature. 3. Do-it-yourself work—Juvenile literature. 4. Physics—Juvenile literature. I. Title.
TS171.57.L43 2015
621—dc23
                                                                                    2014004237

Manufactured in the United States of America

CONTENTS

INTRODUCTION

On the campus of North Carolina State University sits the revolutionary James B. Hunt Jr. Library. It is very much a traditional library in the sense that it contains books, periodicals, and other resources. However, the Hunt Library is also very modern, containing plenty of advanced technology and forward-thinking ideas.

Near the entrance, a huge glass wall reveals eighteen thousand large metal bins soaring four stories high in an enormous warehouse storage room. These bins take the place of the traditional stacks used by most libraries. Users search for titles on a jumbo interactive screen, and bookBots, the library's robotic book delivery devices, scurry around what are called robot alleys pulling books—requested via the central computer screen, personal computers, or handheld devices—out of bins. Library materials are delivered by the bots to the requested areas of the library.

On the second floor of the library is the iPearl Immersion Theater, a digital exhibit space that presents viewers with all the best that NC State has to offer. Interacting with the curved video display, users can scroll through and check out current events on campus. The library's second floor also features group study rooms with web-based video-conferencing capability.

Traveling to the fourth floor brings visitors to the Hunt Library Makerspace, where technology projects that begin as a seed in someone's

The North Carolina State University Makerspace at Hunt Library (www.lib.ncsu.edu/spaces/makerspace) is just one of many makerspaces that have sprung up in the United States.

imagination are brought to vivid, physical life. The makerspace contains a variety of high-tech tools and equipment, such as 3-D printers, laser cutters, and scanners.

The atmosphere and offerings inside the Hunt Library might sound unique, experienced only by someone lucky enough to visit the university's campus in Raleigh. But that just isn't the case. Innovative physical computing technologies, such as the bookBots, have been popping up for some time now. So have the designated areas in which such inventions are thought up and created. These special well-equipped places are called makerspaces—a term that the Hunt Library borrowed for the proper name of its own area for exploring creative technologies.

Makerspaces are essentially just what they sound like—they are "spaces" where people can "make" things. Moving past this basic and obvious definition, one could say that makerspaces are gathering spots where ingenuity takes center stage. They are areas designed for the discussion of ideas, filled with all sorts of awesome equipment that most people can't necessarily afford to purchase for their own individual use.

More important than all the tools and equipment, however, is the human element of makerspaces. Michelle Elbert, an administrator at ATX Hackerspace in Austin, Texas, says, "You can have a hackerspace without a laser. You can have a hackerspace without free Wi-Fi. You might even get away with having a [makerspace] without a dedicated location. But you'll never have one without a community of people."

Chapter 1

A Space to Make Cool Stuff

Since the beginning of time, there have been spaces of some sort where people could make things. Back in the day, these spaces were usually called woodworking or metal-working shops. Even the family barn or garage could serve as a creative space. Magazines published in the early twentieth century urged citizens to make creative changes to technologies such as the radio and automobiles. "Publications from that era are filled with articles of how to turn your Model T into a farm truck, into a camper, etc.," says Jeff Crews, director of the maker-space Splat Space in Durham, North Carolina. Attitudes about the ability of

Wood shop classes can be considered early makerspaces. Today's makerspaces can have the same types of tools as a wood shop, but they also feature high-tech equipment and gadgets.

everyday people to create changed pretty quickly, though. Crews notes that by the middle of the century, "there was this feeling that technology had gotten so complicated that only experts could deal with it."

Do-It-Yourself Makes a Comeback

In the early 2000s, people started feeling the need to explore and create again, to design things and to make their own "stuff." They didn't want to just have to rely on what they could purchase at the nearby big-box store. Experts seem to think that the Internet had a lot to do with this new wave of creativity. The web lets people freely share their ideas and designs with others. For instance, someone who wants to learn how to shingle a house

File   Edit   View   Favorites   Tools   Help

HACKER SCOUTS

Hacker Scouts

Hacker Scouts is an organization created by Samantha and Chris Cook in 2012 in Oakland, California. The Cooks decided to start the organization because they wanted to give kids a place where they could create things. Kids ages four to fifteen are invited to be part of the organization. Younger children up to age eight are part of the Sparks program, while kids ages eight to fifteen are part of the Guild program. Projects in the programs are geared to each individual age group.

Participants can earn patches when they complete various types of projects. For example, a "Dumpster Diving" patch is given to members when they make things out of repurposed materials. Patches are also awarded when participants learn a new skill, such as soldering.

In 2013, the Boy Scouts of America insisted that the organization change its name because the name was too similar to its own. In order to avoid legal issues, the organization's name was changed to Curiosity Hacked.

can go online and find a free instructional video on YouTube created by a roofing expert. Likewise, a person interested in finding out how to make a fancy wreath for his or her front door can do a quick search on Pinterest and find a variety of interesting options, complete with photos and step-by-step instructions. Such project searches even apply to physical computing. If, for instance, someone decided to create a plastic snowflake using a 3-D printer, there would be dozens of designs to choose from on various project-sharing websites.

The do-it-yourself (DIY) movement has become so popular in the twenty-first century that along with many online resources available on the subject, there are also print magazines and entire television networks dedicated to it as well. The online and print version of *MAKE* magazine is considered a

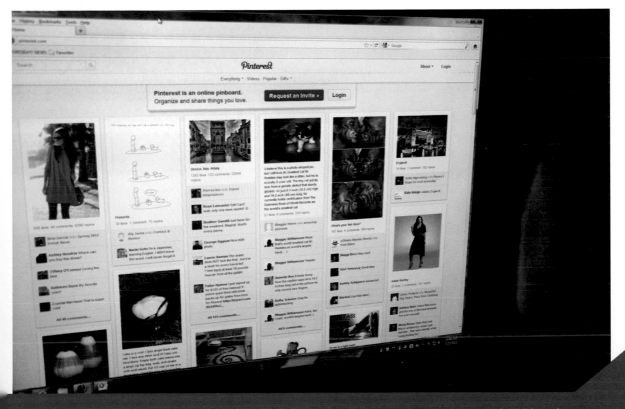

Pinterest (www.pinterest.com) is an online resource where people can share project ideas by "pinning" them to their categorized walls. Pinterest was founded by Ben Silbermann. In August 2010, there were only five thousand users. By April 2012, there were well over seventeen million.

jackpot of ideas for makers. It has a "cookbook" of DIY projects for the garage, for the kitchen, for the workshop, and for the backyard. There are instructions for building a robot, designing and constructing a rocket, making an FM transmitter, mixing up cider at the kitchen table, making a guitar out of license plates and random scraps of wood, and much more. Projects range from easy to difficult and generally include step-by-step instructions and how-to videos.

How Makerspaces Fit In

Dedicated makerspaces started to appear on the scene around 2005. That is also when *MAKE* magazine was founded and the term "makerspace" was officially coined. Prior to that time, there were only places called hackerspaces that were primarily focused on electronic equipment and projects.

File   Edit   View   Favorites   Tools   Help

WHAT'S IN A NAME?

What's in a Name?

These types of spaces go by many different names, including makerspaces, hackerspaces, and fab labs. True makerspaces tend to be larger in size, scope, and offerings than hackerspaces. The smallest of all the spaces, fab labs are generally found in educational institutions. They have very limited equipment and are usually free to members of the organization in which they're found.

Regardless of the name, these places have one goal in mind: to give people a place where they can design, invent, and create, either on their own or as a collaborative effort with others. For convenience, though, the term "makerspaces" will be the term used most in this book.

As time went on, makerspaces continued to be like their hackerspace cousins in that they were places where people could find high-tech electronic equipment. But in addition to those offerings, makerspaces also added other tools and equipment to the mix so that people could create projects in other creative disciplines, such as woodworking, crafting, metalworking, cooking, and textiles.

Physical Computing

Today's makerspaces are filled with machinery and technology that could have been created in these types of workspaces. A number of these high-tech tools operate using computer hardware and software. Controlling

Advanced physical computing equipment, such as the computerized lathe seen here, can be found in many makerspaces.

machines and other three-dimensional objects using computers is known as physical computing.

Computers are also part of projects that members of makerspaces create. Computer microcontrollers such as Arduino and applications processors (basically computer chips or tiny computers) such as the Raspberry Pi have a prominent place in makerspaces. They control the physical-world elements, such as lights and motors, of the projects that makers create. In other words, they make things run.

Microcontrollers and microcomputers are examples of how physical computing is connected to the makerspace movement. Other connections include the use of tools such as 3-D printers and computer numerical control (CNC) machines. In CNC machining, computers control certain kinds of machinery or industrial tools, such as mills and grinders.

MYTHS&FACTS

MYTH The makerspace movement is only for adults.

FACT Absolutely not! Makerspaces are for everyone. While it is true that some makerspaces must restrict kids and teens from using specific tools and areas, many do allow youth makers to use such items and facilities as long as an adult is with them at all times. Other maker-spaces have specific times that their spaces are made available to kids, teens, and families. Additionally, the online maker movement is entirely open to kids and teens. In fact, DIY.org is specifically geared to youth ages eight to sixteen.

MYTH A lot of money is necessary to become involved in the makerspace movement.

FACT Nothing could be further from the truth. Creating via makerspaces can be done on the cheap. One of the things that this movement encourages is the repurposing of materials. "Dumpster diving" is a celebrated activity with makers. The coolest projects are those that are made using materials someone has already thrown away. So little to no money is even required to be part of this movement.

MYTH Only people who know a lot about science are part of the maker-space movement.

FACT Once again, a decided no. People interested in the movement shouldn't worry if they don't know a lot about science. The maker-space movement is a place where people can learn all about science (plus math, engineering, art, and design) in a fun, hands-on way. They get to create projects and gain in-depth knowledge of these subjects at the same time.

Chapter 2

Getting Those Creative Juices Flowing

In the twenty-first century, the learning model in the United States seems to have changed, at least it has at many educational institutions throughout the country. There seems to be more of an emphasis these days on helping kids and teens become more innovative. Education professionals have come to realize that in order to help students become as successful in their future lives and jobs as they can be, students need to be taught not only the standard subjects, such as math, reading, and science, but also how to solve problems with creative solutions and how to work together with their peers, both in person and online.

That's exactly the type of learning that occurs every day in makerspaces around the world. These spaces encourage hands-on learning and creative problem solving. As Aaron Birenboim of Quelab, a makerspace in Albuquerque, New Mexico, states, "Makerspaces are based on a new type of learning that is much more adaptive and faster....We teach you enough to be safe and then encourage you to get started. From there, you can do your own experimentation and collaboration with peers to learn what needs to be done to meet your goals."

The main purpose of makerspaces is to encourage collaboration. Competition is not that common at makerspaces. Instead, people want to work together to help each other figure out solutions for their projects and ideas.

Makerspaces are based on the idea that collaboration is highly important—that two minds, or maybe three or four, are definitely better than one. Teamwork is an important part of the makerspace experience. One makerspace director compares working with others in a creative space to having a workout partner at a gym. Other innovators provide motivation, help others work through difficult tasks, and celebrate when everything goes right and a project is a success.

File   Edit   View   Favorites   Tools   Help

CHATTING WITH AN EXPERT

Chatting with an Expert

Mark Huson is cofounder of Baltimore Node, a member-run makerspace in Baltimore, Maryland. The following are excerpts from a question-and-answer session with him about makerspaces.

What are the greatest benefits for people who get involved in the makerspace movement?

Community is number one by far. The space needs members to operate. In order for the space to exist, the people need to want to be there. Makerspaces also provide people with tools and space that are otherwise too expensive or impractical for one person to attain alone.

What are the coolest projects that have been created at Baltimore Node?

One of my favorites is the Low D project, which consists of an LED light sign made of programmable Christmas lights. Another is the life-size replica of Han Solo made in carbonite. We've helped local art students make a drum that drums to each step made with a special pair of shoes across the world.

How can kids and teens get involved in the makerspace movement?

Find a local one and drop by. Talk to your local library about setting aside a room to form a mini makerspace. Libraries all over are looking to capitalize on the maker movement, and it helps them solve this need when you rent or reserve a space from them.

CHATTING WITH AN EXPERT

How do you think the makerspace movement could affect the future?
One possible way is by making expensive tools more accessible. As 3-D printers become more well known and people realize what can be done quickly and easily on a laser cutter or shopbot, I see more local manufacturing being done. In the same way Walmart does just-in-time delivery for goods, people can have just-in-time goods made locally.

If at First You Don't Succeed...

Makerspaces encourage mistakes. That might sound odd at first because most schools—and many businesses for that matter—train people to avoid making mistakes. But in a makerspace environment, mistakes are not viewed as failures by any means. In fact, errors are actually celebrated because they are part of the process that helps people get closer to their goals. They can learn from their mistakes, which lets them change the way they approach a problem and come to a successful conclusion.

To understand this "mistakes-are-great" philosophy a little better, think of Thomas Edison, one of the greatest inventors and innovators who ever lived. During his lifetime, he created such world-changing inventions as the phonograph, the lightbulb, the motion picture, and the alkaline battery. His inventions didn't happen overnight. Mistakes, or as some people would call them, "failures," were all part of the game. In the biography *Edison: His Life and Inventions*, Edison's friend Water S. Mallory recalls seeing the inventor conducting battery experiments. Realizing that Edison had spent hours testing battery cells and had not had much luck, Mallory said it was a shame that Edison had not gotten the results he had hoped to get from all the failed

Thomas Edison is shown here in his lab. Had Edison lived today, chances are good he would have been a proponent, if not a frequent user, of makerspaces.

experiments. Edison turned to his friend and said, "Results! Why, man, I have gotten a lot of results! I know several thousand things that won't work."

In a way, Edison's lab in Menlo Park, New Jersey, was essentially a type of makerspace. Likewise, makerspaces can be considered the Edison laboratory of the twenty-first century. Who knows what amazing new products will come out of the makerspaces of today and the future!

Made to Order

Generally, makerspaces are tailored to fit the communities they support. For example, if a community really has a need and interest in woodworking,

A group of technology enthusiasts meets for a Raspberry Pi Foundation event at Alpha One Labs in Brooklyn, New York. Makers interested in electronics have plenty of electronics equipment on hand.

then naturally a makerspace in that area will be supplied with equipment such as table saws, routers, chisels, lathes, and related hand tools. If, however, a community has more of an interest in electronic-themed and physical-computing projects, then the makerspace in that area will be outfitted with such things as 3-D printers, laser cutters, soldering equipment, circuitry-building components, and computers with specific high-tech software. Still other makerspaces may have a combination of all these types of tools and equipment because their members have a diverse set of interests.

Since each makerspace is unique, how do people find out if a particular makerspace is the right fit for them? The first recommendation is to visit the space in person and see what it has to offer. While touring the site, it's important to ask specific questions about the space to get a clear understanding of what the environment and community have to offer.

TEN GREAT QUESTIONS

TO ASK A MAKERSPACE OWNER OR OPERATION

1 What kinds of tools and equipment are available at the makerspace?

2 Is there safety training offered on the equipment?

3 How often is the equipment maintained?

4 Are any supplies available, or do I need to bring my own?

5 Can I store my projects at the space?

6 What kinds of classes are offered and how often are they offered?

7 What is the membership fee?

8 What hours is the makerspace open?

9 How many people use the makerspace on a regular basis?

10 Is there a place to chat and brainstorm with other makerspace members?

Chapter 3

Innovation Around the World

Great things are happening at makerspaces in every corner of the world. Research indicates that there are approximately 750 active makerspaces throughout the world, with hundreds more being planned or built. A little less than half of all active makerspaces are located in the United States. The rest are located in more than nineteen countries, including the United Kingdom, Indonesia, Norway, India, Australia, Singapore, Canada, and Brazil.

A Soulful Space in Singapore

The motto of the Sustainable Living Lab (SL2) in Singapore is "Welcome to the makerspace for the soul!" Projects created at SL2 are generally made with materials that have been upcycled, which means old items have been reused and made into better, more environmentally friendly materials. M. Ibnur Rashad, a cofounder at SL2, was quoted in a 2013 article in *Business Times* as saying that upcycling at his makerspace allows makers to "start

Artist Amy Chrisman of Danville, Illinois, sells jewelry made from recycled aluminum at her local farmers' market. Upcycling is a great way to help the environment.

seeing waste as a key strategic resource and we start living more thoughtfully with the intent to minimize environmental impact."

Some of the awesome upcycled items created at SL2 include: speakers made out of bamboo called iBam2, which are designed for use with various Apple products (iPhone, iPad, etc.); children's toy blocks, lamp shades, and stools made out of cast-off cardboard; key chains, luggage tags, and diary covers made out of fire hoses that are no longer in use; and spoons, boxes, and spatulas made out of worn-out wooden planks.

Digital Jewelry and Boathouses in Scotland

The makerspace movement is also alive and well at MAKLab in Glasgow, Scotland. According to founding director Bruce Newlands, MAKLab's greatest benefit to the Glasgow community is the fact that it offers "low cost and free access to a variety of technologies and training opportunities to everyone and anyone." Workshops are offered for both adults and children.

MAKLab is equipped with 3-D printers and scanners, a laser cutter/engraver, milling machines and routers, a vinyl cutter, a vacuum former (to create packaging and molds), and a wide selection of electronics components. The equipment is in such high demand that members are expected to book time on machines before they arrive to create.

Since opening in 2012, this makerspace has helped people conduct research, explore creative projects, and even start businesses. Some of the coolest projects created at MAKLab include digital jewelry, the framework for a public boathouse built on the Isle of Tiree, and electronics that use light to transmit data.

Creating All Day, Every Day in Winnipeg

AssentWorks is a nonprofit maker lab in Winnipeg, Canada, that is run solely by volunteers. Even the space's founders do not take a salary. A fabulous feature of this particular makerspace is the fact that it's open twenty-four hours a day, seven days a week. Members are able to come in at a time that works best for them. Cofounder David Bernhardt notes that the space's busiest time is between 8 PM and 3 AM

Bernhardt believes that AssentWorks "has brought together many communities within our community." The makerspace has worked with various academic institutes and start-up communities and has brought together maker members with local businesspeople and tech workers. Bernhardt is also proud of the way AssentWorks has been able to show local government officials, and the public at large, the power of maker communities.

The many interesting projects created at AssentWorks include parts used to assemble the Urbee, a car made up mostly of parts that were printed on a 3-D printer. Other AssentWorks projects include a giant, fully functional old-school camera, complete with bellows, and the prototypes, or models, for products sold by the start-up company Home Snowboards.

Pictured above is the framework for a boathouse created by MAKLab on Scotland's Isle of Tiree.

Urbee creator Jim Kor displays his car at an event in France. The Urbee was built using parts generated using 3-D printing technology.

Many Tools for Many People in Ohio

The Columbus Idea Foundry (CIF) is a makerspace located in Ohio. This program, started by Alex Bandar, moved into its 60,000 square foot (5,575 square meter) industrial space in April 2014. Projects undertaken at CIF have included blacksmithing, laser cutting, and CNC machining. "CNC" stands for computer numerical control. In CNC machining, computers control certain kinds of machinery or industrial tools such as mills and grinders.

The offerings at CIF are extensive, which may be the reason many different types of people are attracted to the space. Members include artists, engineers, web developers, product developers, and businesspeople, or, as Bandar describes them, "creative people with an idea who are looking for the knowledge of how to create it or the tools to make it happen."

Cool projects to come out of CIF include an electric motorcycle, a suite of hybrid cars, a computer-based system to grow food in water instead of soil, and a line of magnetic laser-cut gears "that can make any magnetic surface into a mechanical laboratory," according to Bandar.

File   Edit   View   Favorites   Tools   Help

CHATTING WITH AN EXPERT

Chatting with an Expert

David Bernhardt is the director at AssentWorks in Winnipeg, Canada.

How do you feel places like AssentWorks helps kids and teens become more innovative?

I believe strongly in a positive correlation between working together and innovation. There are many innovative people working in their basement alone. Places like AW bring them out and expose them (for better or worse). With the younger generation, we are now experiencing the age where the digital world creates physical things. Finishing a video game is kind of rewarding, but making a digital 3-D (CAD) object, then 3-D printing it or CNCing it is awesome! We have parents who are becoming members, just so their kids can hang out with other makers. We have kids who are ten years old designing things, and their parents come and use the tools to make it (as per our insurance policy). At one time, our youngest member was eighteen and oldest was eighty-eight. Now that's awesome!

CONTINUE ON NEXT PAGE...

File   Edit   View   Favorites   Tools   Help

CONTINUE....CHATTING WITH AN EXPERT

What are the greatest benefits people can have by becoming involved in the makerspace movement in general?
The maker community brings together an assortment of people you would not find anywhere else. By being involved, you are writing the future. There are many groups that gather to discuss ideas and solutions, where a maker community is about the action. Without action, there is no movement.

How do you feel makerspaces like AssentWorks will affect the future?
Makerspaces will be changing everything in the future. Everything from manufacturing, business start-ups, enabling ideas, education systems, how we buy things will be affected by makerspaces. Indiegogo and Kickstarter are a great example of the impact of makerspaces and communities. Also communities don't refer to a specific geographical location anymore. We have community members from around the world.

Creative in Seattle

Walk down Broadway in Seattle's Capitol Hill area and you'll come across Metrix Create: Space. This makerspace contains all sorts of interesting equipment, such as CNC routing machines, 3-D printers, and an advanced circuit lab. Members can take classes in laser cutting and etching and 3-D printing, among other areas.

All ages are welcome at Metrix Create: Space. One workshop that both children and adults enjoy happens on Monday nights. It's the "Hack

File Edit View Favorites Tools Help

ONE MAKER'S TAKE ON THE SITUATION

One Maker's Take on the Situation

Alex Bandar, the founder and director of the Columbus Idea Foundry, has an interesting take on why makerspaces such as his have become so popular and successful: people need to create in a community atmosphere. That role was filled by shop classes in schools years ago. Little by little, shop classes were replaced by computer labs in the 1980s and 1990s, "if they were replaced at all," he says.

Bandar adds that while computer labs are a good thing, "we need the next generation of designers, engineers, and product developers to both know how to design and program machines *as well as* how to build for them. If you know how tools work, you design much better for them."

As for the future of makerspaces, Bandar believes that they will continue to be important places where people everywhere can gather to brainstorm and use cutting-edge technology to create a variety of things.

"Just think of that," says Bandar. "Instead of a tiny pie slice of the total global talent producing the engineering components, software apps, and retail goods for the rest of the world, we can have seven billion educated and empowered problem solvers designing and producing whatever they can think of. To me, that's an extremely exciting horizon."

Your Own Clothes" class, where makers can use the space's sewing machines, embroidery machines, sergers, and knitting machines to create one-of-a-kind apparel. Groups of Hacker Scouts gather at the space twice a month to create anything from biodomes to LED arrays.

Live Free (and Creatively) or Die in New Hampshire

New Hampshire's first makerspace, MakeIt Labs, is located in the town of Nashua. It proclaims on its website that "If you like making cool stuff, you're in the right place." According to Adam Shrey at MakeIt Labs, the most popular workshops offered at the space are the welding, CNC plasma cutting, electronics, and Arduino-related classes. And, the "automotive lift is one of our biggest draws as are the welders, the CNC plasma cutter, and the 3-D printers." MakeIt Labs members are encouraged to get their kids involved at the space—with adult supervision, of course. "We also offer discounts to students who are interested in the space or the classes." Some of the coolest projects made at MakeIt Labs include the trailer that was converted into a food truck and an organized group project where a team of makers converted a Kawasaki Ninja 250 into an electric motorcycle.

A Passionate Parachute in New Mexico

The makerspace movement is growing quickly in New Mexico, thanks to makerspaces such as the Parachute Factory. The space was built on owner Mariano Ulibarri's belief that makerspaces should support people's "passion projects" by allowing them to explore and test their creative sides in ways that make sense for them.

The Parachute Factory attracts makers of all ages, from kids all the way to grandparents. Members also come from many different backgrounds. "On any given day at Parachute Factory, you might find artists, athletes, scientists, farmers, video-game enthusiasts, or bookworms tinkering away," says Ulibarri. "The common thread that seems to pull all of these people together is a strong sense of curiosity and a desire to solve problems in creative ways."

Interesting projects made in the space include a giant Nintendo that runs on the computer programming platforms Raspberry Pi and MaKey MaKey. One of the Parachute Factory's most popular programs is "Fix It

A member of the Parachute Factory helps a young child use the space's equipment. Makerspaces are about community and are welcoming to creators encompassing a variety of generations.

Friday," where makerspace members help fix broken items that people bring in from their homes.

Ulibarri would like to see more schools become involved in the maker-space movement. Until then, he'll have to settle for making inroads in other ways that may help students create. Future plans call for the Parachute Factory to help several public libraries throughout the state establish maker programs of their own.

31

Chapter 4

Making Your Own Space

Teens and preteens looking to scratch a creative itch would do well to follow the advice given by Mariano Ulibarri of the Parachute Factory: "Find a local makerspace and join!" But what if there isn't a makerspace open in their community? Ulibarri has an answer for that as well. "If one doesn't exist," he says, "grab a group of like-minded friends and start one up."

So, how does one go about becoming a maker-space founder? How would a person even get started? Well, the first—and best—step is to consult with people who have already started makerspaces themselves. There's no reason to rein-vent the wheel when others

Hundreds of participants attend a Massachusetts conference on "How to Make a Makerspace." Those who want to be makerspace founders should learn from established makerspace heads.

have already been there and done that and can give others their top tips regarding makerspace success.

More Advice from the Experts

Many of the experts interviewed for this book had great advice for budding makerspace founders. Just about all of them agreed that the first thing a person should do is organize the people who will be coming to the space. As Ulibarri says, "The biggest resource that you need to get a successful makerspace going is people. Tap into your local DIY community early."

Students gather around the laser cutter at the Parachute Factory. Young people don't have to wait for a makerspace to come to their community; they can start their own.

Jeff Crews from Splat Space seconds that advice. "Start small and grow organically," says Crews. He recommends advertising at local spots where possible members might be, such as libraries. Posting that a new makerspace is getting started on sites such as Meetup is also an option.

Room to Grow

Once a group of interested people has been found, it's time to hold a meeting or two in a free space—again, libraries are good spots, if they have public meeting rooms—to discuss actually renting a physical space. Rushing to rent a space and a bunch of tools without knowing for sure if there will be enough members to pay the dues, which pay the rental bills, is not the best idea.

Alex Bandar suggests meeting in someone's garage or living room for up to a year or more, until there are enough people interested in being members. He also advises that makerspace founders should act as responsible entrepreneurs and put together a solid business plan so that they can know where they're going and what they want to accomplish with their space.

Once a group of committed makers has been identified and a business plan is in place, it is time for founders to look into renting the space and the equipment. This is where a community of people will really help. Founders should find out what most of the people in their group are interested in, which will help organizers figure out the best type of equipment and tools to get for the space. Ulibarri warns founders to not spend a small fortune on gear—at least not at first. "That is the biggest pitfall a new makerspace can make," he says. "You don't need a fancy 3-D printer or laser cutter to get started—those things will come as you need them."

Mark Huson of Baltimore Node agrees. As founder of the Node and an advisor on another makerspace called the Baltimore Factory, he recommends "starting small with a reasonable budget." The size of a makerspace should make sense in terms of how many members it has.

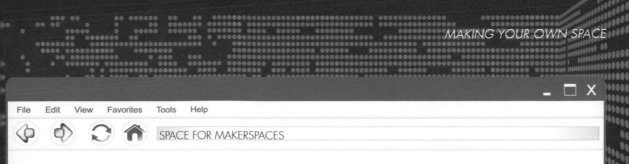

File   Edit   View   Favorites   Tools   Help

SPACE FOR MAKERSPACES

Space for Makerspaces

Makerspaces come in all shapes and sizes. At the most basic level, they can be found in tiny one-room locations in a small or big city where barely one or two computers and a 3-D printer are able to squeeze inside. Those that are slightly larger and more organized might set up shop in enormous warehouses that are divided into separate cubicles so that dozens of projects can be worked on and stored at the same time.

Some makerspaces are found in multipurpose or conference rooms in libraries—just like the one-room makerspace at the North Carolina State University campus. Other makerspaces are found in old factory districts, tucked in between cafes and restaurants on a busy main street, inside middle schools and high schools, and in shopping malls.

There are even some makerspaces that are portable. Some innovators have found that old eighteen-wheeler shipping containers from the trucking industry make ideal movable makerspaces. These big rectangular boxes, which can be outfitted with all kinds of cool tools and equipment, are leased by libraries and schools. They set up in a parking lot until they are scurried away to the next location. Now that shows just how creative makers can be!

Making Use of Existing Space

Makerspace founders looking to find a meeting space should talk to someone at their local library or community center. These places may have an extra room in the building that is going unused that they would like to rent out. Also, maybe they'd like to start attracting more people to their space. Many libraries, in particular, have seen a decline in patrons since so much

Meeting in a room or free space in a library can be a good first step for makerspace founders.

information can be attained through the online world. Setting up a maker-space in such a location could be the answer for both the place with the extra room and the members looking for a space.

In a way, starting a makerspace in a library is a genius idea because it helps draw in the community, getting people involved in lifelong learning in creative, innovative ways. Of course, library-based makerspaces probably can't offer loud and messy equipment like woodworking and metalworking tools, mainly because there would be too much noise. But other types of interesting devices, such as 3-D printers, computers, soldering equipment, and laser cutters—or simply tables filled with interesting supplies, such as duct tape, knitting needles, and yarn—could be tools available in such a space.

Finding the Money

Funding for makerspaces can come in a variety of ways. Some makerspaces have "tool drives," where they ask members of the community to donate equipment that they're no longer using. Some makerspaces also conduct fund-raisers by having members sell the items that they make.

Another idea is to invite local companies and organizations to Mini Maker Faires so that makers can show off their work. This might inspire many

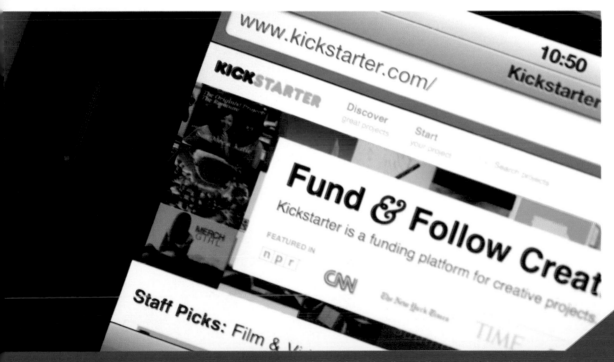

The Kickstarter website (www.kickstarter.com) claims it is the "world's largest funding platform for creative projects." People raise thousands of dollars for their organizations every year through this system.

of the visiting executives of local businesses to donate funds to the cause. Schools and libraries can also apply for grants offered by federal and state agencies. Also, any makerspace—small or large—can take advantage of the recent phenomenon of crowdsourcing, where groups go online to ask people for donations to support their projects and causes.

Making It Happen

Alex Bandar has expressed an interesting viewpoint, one that many people who think they may want to become makerspace founders may not think about when they decide to start their own space. "The first thing to note is that people who start a makerspace actually cease being makers and instead become administrators, fund-raisers, accountants, promoters, maintenance people, and more. You will do everything *except* make stuff. If that's something you're interested in, go for it! If it isn't, then leave the makerspace founding to someone more interested in running a business than building new products."

Yet the experts interviewed here all agree that people who really do want to become founders, or simply become members in an existing makerspace community, should definitely do it. After all, what can be cooler than coming up with ideas and designs, devising plans, working through a step-by-step process, and then creating something new and totally awesome?

Innovation is life changing. Making stuff oneself is amazing and rewarding. Who knows? Maybe something created by a makerspace member could become just as valuable to the world as inventions made by famous innovators of the past. People who participate in makerspaces and the do-it-yourself movement could be the next Thomas Edison. The only way to find out is to get out there and start innovating.

Makerspaces are just the place to get moving in the proper—in other words, innovative—direction. The makerspace movement train is at the station. Creative, curious people would be smart to climb aboard and find out for themselves what this fascinating cultural phenomenon is all about.

GLOSSARY

bot A computerized machine that can do the work of a person; short for "robot."

circuitry The parts (like resistors, transistors, capacitors, inductors, and diodes) that are needed to make an electronic circuit.

coin To create a new name, word, or term.

crowdsourcing The practice of getting the funding, services, or help you need from a large group of people, generally via the Internet.

etch To create a picture or pattern by cutting into a surface of glass or metal.

fab lab A small-scale, do-it-yourself workshop that offers digital fabrication.

hackerspace A workspace operated by a community of like-minded people that contains tools and equipment and offers classes in the discipline of computer or digital technology.

laser cutter A technology that uses a laser to cut materials.

lathe A machine tool that is used in metalworking, woodturning, etc., for sanding, cutting, drilling, and facing.

Maker Faire A "show and tell" event where people showcase the things they have made at various makerspaces.

microcontroller A very small computer that controls a machine or other device.

myth An idea that is believed by many people to be true, even though it is not.

solder The act of joining metals together by melting lead or tin over them to create a bond or joint.

sustainable Describes something that can be used without being all used up.

textile Having to do with fabric or weaving.

3-D printer A printer that is capable of making three-dimensional objects out of a variety of materials.

upcycle Using old, already used materials to create something new and usually even better than the original.

FOR MORE INFORMATION

AssentWorks
125 Adelaide Street
Winnipeg, MB R3A 0A3
Canada
(204) 943-7909
Website: http://assentworks.ca
AssentWorks was founded by three entrepreneurs whose main goal was to
    help other entrepreneurs start their dream businesses by providing
    equipment and removing barriers associated with start-ups. This non-
    profit fabrication lab is run solely by volunteers—not even the founders
    draw salaries from it. Free tours of the facilities are offered generally on
    Tuesdays, but contact the space ahead of time to confirm availability.

Columbus Idea Foundry (CIF)
421 West State Street
Columbus, OH 43215
(614) 893 6053
Website: http://columbusideafoundry.com
Columbus Idea Foundry is currently the largest makerspace in the world. This
    space offers free tours of its facilities for business groups, educational
    field trips, and clubs. Scheduling in advance is highly recommended.

Curiosity Hacked
c/o School Factory
161 W. Wisconsin Avenue, #2
Milwaukee, WI 53203
Website: http://www.hacker-scouts.org
Curiosity Hacked (formerly Hacker Scouts) is a national nonprofit organiza-
    tion that stresses STEM education and the arts. The organization offers

open-source materials and support programs that enable young makers to build their skills and achieve their maker dreams.

Maker Education Initiative
1001 42nd Street, Suite 230
Oakland, CA 94608
Website: http://www.makered.org
The Maker Education Initiative creates opportunities for young people to tap into their individual and collective creativity, while fostering their interest in science, technology, engineering, math, art, and learning as a whole through making. The initiative is responsible for a number of maker programs, including Maker Corps.

Maker Media, Inc.
1005 Gravenstein Highway North
Sebastopol, CA 95472
(707) 829-1154
Website: http://makermedia.com
Maker Media publishes *Make* magazine, launched in 2005. The organization has also been instrumental in the conceptualization of the Maker Faire, first held in 2006, and is at the forefront of the movement to bring makerspaces to schools through the Young Makers program.

New Jersey Maker Association
35 Berrue Circle
Piscataway Township, NJ 08854
Website: http://makerspace.rutgers.edu
The New Jersey Makerspace Association provides guidance for prospective makerspace founders, private and public. Affiliated with Rutgers

University, the association helps makerspaces apply for grants that support events and purchase equipment, as well as promote these spaces throughout the state.

New Mexico Highlands University Media Technology Department
1005 Diamond Street
Las Vegas, NM 87701
(505) 425-7511
Website: http://www.nmhu.edu
The mission of the media arts program at New Mexico Highlands University is to educate students in technical skills, as well as inspire them to work creatively and collaboratively. The department has a great reputation in the museum technology industry regarding its support of makerspaces.

Websites

Due to the changing nature of Internet links, Rosen Publishing has developed an online list of websites related to the subject of this book. This site is updated regularly. Please use the following link to access the list:

http://www.rosenlinks.com/DIL/maker

FOR FURTHER READING

Anderson, Chris. *Makers: The New Industrial Revolution*. New York, NY: Crown Business, 2012.

Cohen, Jacob. *Getting the Most Out of Makerspaces to Build Robots*. New York, NY: Rosen Publishing, 2014.

Gabrielson, Curt. *Tinkering: Kids Learn by Making Stuff*. Sebastopol, CA: Maker Media, Inc., 2013.

Hatch, Mark. *The Maker Movement Manifesto: Rules for Innovation in the New World of Crafters, Hackers, and Tinkerers*. New York, NY: McGraw-Hill, 2013.

Honey, Margaret, and David E. Kanter. *Design, Make, and Play: Growing the Next Generation of STEM Innovators*. New York, NY: Routledge, 2013.

Kemp, Adam. *The Makerspace Workbench: Tools, Technologies, and Techniques for Making*. Sebastopol, CA: Maker Media, Inc., 2013.

Lang, David. *Zero to Maker: Learn (Just Enough) to Make (Just About) Anything*. Sebastopol, CA: Maker Media, Inc., 2013.

Martinez, Sylvia Libow, and Gary Stager. *Invent to Learn: Making, Tinkering, and Engineering in the Classroom*. Torrance, CA: Constructing Modern Knowledge Press, 2013.

Petrikowski, Nicki Peter. *Getting the Most Out of Makerspaces to Create with 3-D Printers*. New York, NY: Rosen Publishing, 2014.

Rauf, Don. *Getting the Most Out of Makerspaces to Explore Arduino and Electronics*. New York, NY: Rosen Publishing, 2014.

Roslund, Samantha, and Emily Puckett Rodgers. *Makerspaces*. North Mankato, MN: Cherry Lake Publishing, 2013.

Wilkinson, Karen, and Mike Petrich. *The Art of Tinkering*. San Francisco, CA: Weldon Owen, 2014.

BIBLIOGRAPHY

Aquino, Judith. "Thomas Edison's 31 Greatest Inventions." Business Insider.
    Retrieved December 16, 2013 (http://www.businessinsider.com/
    thomas-edison-inventions-light-bulb-and-30-more).

Bandar, Alex. Columbus Idea Foundry, Columbus, OH. Personal interview
    with author, December 2013.

Bernhardt, David. Assentworks, Winnipeg, Canada. Personal interview with
    author, December 2013.

Birenboim, Aaron. QueLab, Albuquerque, NM. Personal interview with
    author, December 2013.

Chiang, Susan. "Green Makeovers." *Singapore Business Times*, 2013.
    Retrieved December 16, 2013. (http://www.businesstimes.com
    .sg/archive/monday/lifestyle/shopping/green-makeovers-
    20130105).

Cole, Ian. FamiLAB, Tampa, FL. Personal interview with the author,
    December 2013.

Crews, Jeff. Splat Space, Durham, NC. Personal interview with author,
    December 2013.

Dyer, Frank Lewis. *Edison: His Life and Inventions*. New York, NY: Harper
    Brothers, 1910. Retrieved December 16, 2013 (http://www
    .gutenberg.org/files/820/820-h/820-h.htm).

Elbert, Michelle. ATX Hackerspace, Austin, TX. Personal interview with
    author, December 2013.

Huson, Mark. Baltimore Node, Baltimore, MD. Personal interview with
    author, December 2013.

Makerspace Team. *Makerspace Playbook*. Spring 2013. Retrieved December
    16, 2013 (http://makerspace.com/maker-news/makerspace-playbook).

Newlands, Bruce. MAKLab, Glasgow, Scotland. Personal interview with
    author, December 2013.

New Media Consortium. "NMC on the Horizon: Makerspaces." (Video.)

NMC.org, 2013. Retrieved December 16, 2013 (http://www.nmc .org/events/horizon-makerspaces).

Shrey, Adam. MakeIt Labs, Nashua, NH. Personal interview with author, December 2013.

Swaminathan, Veera. Sustainable Living Lab (SL2), Singapore. Personal Interview with the author. December 2013.

Thomas A. Edison Foundation. "Thomas Edison's Most Famous Inventions." Retrieved December 16, 2013 (http://www.thomasedison.org/index .php/education/inventions).

Tilton, Sky. Metrix Create: Space, Seattle, WA. Personal interview with author, December 2013.

Ulibarri, Mariano. Parachute Factory, Las Vegas, NM. Personal interview with author, December 2013.

Weissenburger, Rachel. Edison Papers Project, Rutgers University. Correspondence with author, December 2013.

INDEX

About the Author

A graduate of Brigham Young University, Amie Jane Leavitt is an accomplished author and researcher who has written more than fifty books for young people. She has also taught several subjects at various grade levels in both public and private schools.

Photo Credits

Cover and p. 1 (left), p. 11 Monkey Business Images/Shutterstock.com; cover and p. 1 (center left), p. 37 © iStockphoto.com/SeanShot; cover and p. 1 (center right) © iStockphoto.com/monkeybusinessimages; cover and p. 1 (right), pp. 31, 33 © The Parachute Factory; p. 5 Courtesy Brent Brafford, NCSU Libraries; p. 7 FPG/Archive Photos/Getty Images; p. 9 Karen Bleier /AFP/Getty Images; p. 15 Goodluz/Shutterstock.com; p. 18 Education Images/Universal Images Group/Getty Images; p. 19 © Alpha One Labs; p. 23 © AP Images; p. 25 © Sebb Hathaway/Tog Studio; p. 26 Joel Saget /AFP/Getty Images; p. 32 The Boston Globe/Getty Images; p. 36 © iStock-photo.com/SimmiSimons; cover (background) and interior page graphics © iStockphoto.com/suprun.

Designer: Nicole Russo; Editor: Jeanne Nagle; Photo Researcher: Marty Levick